THE BRAVEST LION

by Kristen Griffin

illustrated by Abbey Bryant

Remarkable Books Co. • Houston, Texas

Text and illustrations copyright © 2021 Kristen Griffin
Illustrations by Abbey Bryant
Design by Joe Fahey
All rights reserved.

No part of this book may be reproduced in any manner without express written consent of the publisher, except in the case of brief excerpts in critical reviews and articles. All inquiries or sales requests should be addressed to:

Remarkable Books Co.
kristen@remarkablebooks.com
www.remarkablebooks.com
Remarkable Books Co. • Houston, Texas

Printed and bound in the United States of America
First Edition
10 9 8 7 6 5 4 3 2 1
LCCN 2021913216
ISBN 978-0-578-94530-9

This book was proudly produced by Book Bridge Press
www.bookbridgepress.com

To my family, my amazing husband, and
my two wonderful, crazy, rambunctious
girls, who inspire me every day.
—K. G.

To Elizabeth & Jordan:
I hope you always remember
how special you are!
Be Brave! Be You!!
♡ Kristy

Lions are king of the wild.

They are fierce,

brave, and full of pride.

Do you feel wild and ferocious like a lion,

but have a hard time being brave?

Being brave takes practice.

Sometimes it looks like falling down and getting back up.

And falling down
and getting back up again.

Sometimes friends will encourage you to be brave.

Things may happen that make you want to roar!

Fear is that funny feeling you get in your stomach.
Don't worry. Everyone gets it.

Courage is being brave even when you feel afraid. Sometimes courage sounds like "I'm sorry."

It's normal to be anxious or afraid. Even the toughest lions have a hard time being brave sometimes.

It takes courage to speak up for yourself and others.

That's how you grow and change the world for the better.

Sometimes it is easier to pretend to be something else.
But it takes true courage to be yourself.

Stand tall. Have pride.

You are amazing and one of a kind.